Ruins *of* Rome I

FROM THE COLOSSEUM
TO THE ROMAN FORUM

LAINE CUNNINGHAM

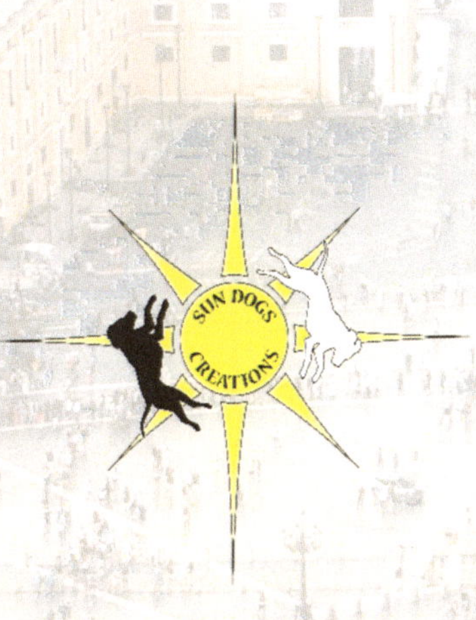

Ruins of Rome I
From the Colosseum to the Roman Forum
A Travel Photo Art Book

Published by Sun Dogs Creations
Changing the World One Book at a Time
Softcover ISBN: 9781946732392
Hardcover ISBN: 9781946732408

Cover Design by Angel Leya

Introduction

At over 2,500 years old, Rome is more than the capital of Italy. It is the center of artistic creativity and a cultural complex that arguably outstrips any other location on earth. Ancient monuments like the Colosseum continue to capture our attention while institutions like the Vatican Museums spur intellectual interest.

The heartbeat of Rome is found in every visitor's soul. The rushing crowds on the main avenues can be left behind by ducking down a side street. After a block or two, enter one of the small neighborhood streets where children play ball and the splash of fountains echoes against the buildings.

From Aventine Hill to St. Peter's Basilica, from the banks of the Tiber to the Aniene, Rome is a kaleidoscopic journey through time.

The photos in *Ruins of Rome I & II* were taken at Palazzo Senatorio, Saint Peter's Basilica and Vatican City, Via della Conciliazione, the Colosseum, Palatine Hill, the Roman Forum, the Pantheon, San Paolo fuori le mura, Piazza del Popolo, Villa Borghese, various obelisks, and other sites. Each collection reproduces the photos at the size of a standard cellphone screen to replicate the experience of being there.

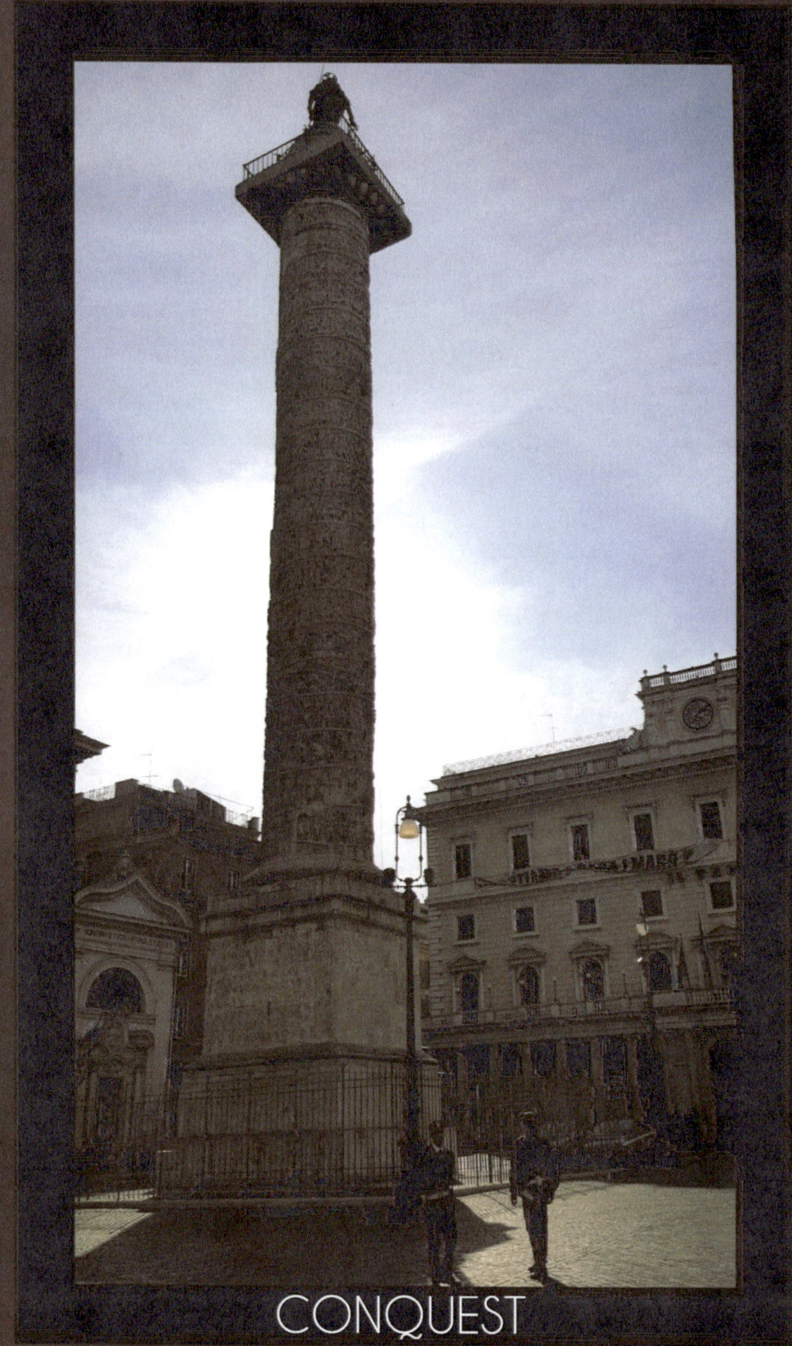

CONQUEST

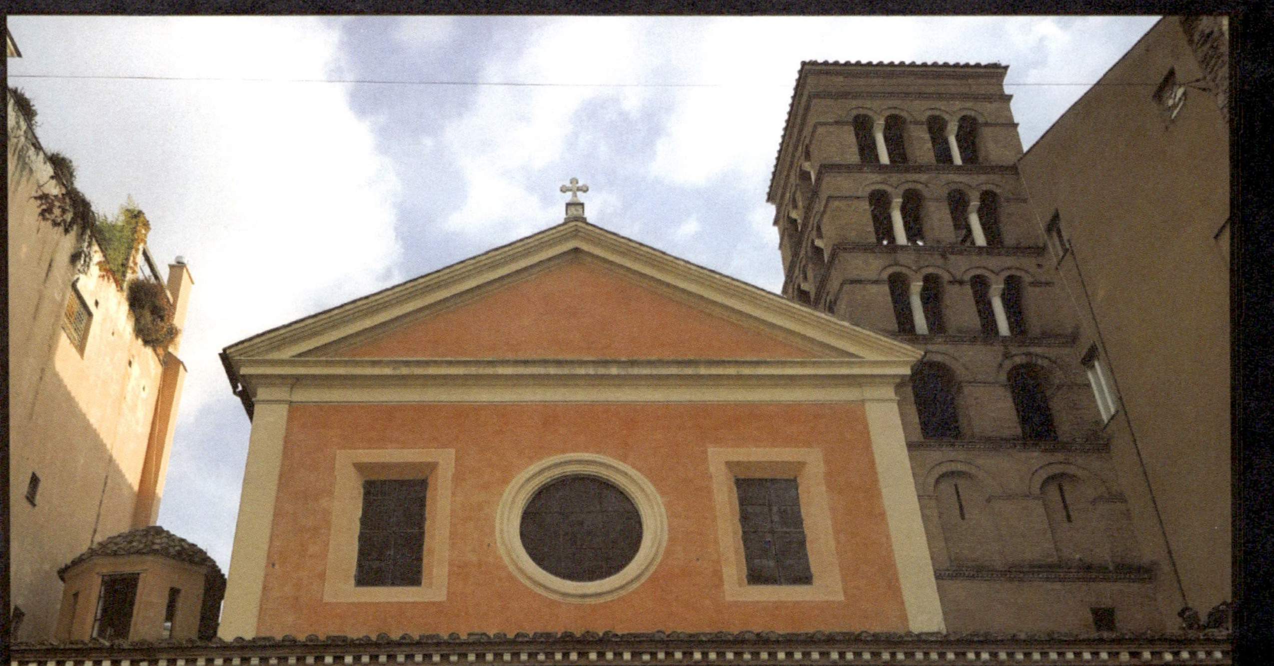

TERMINAL VELOCITY

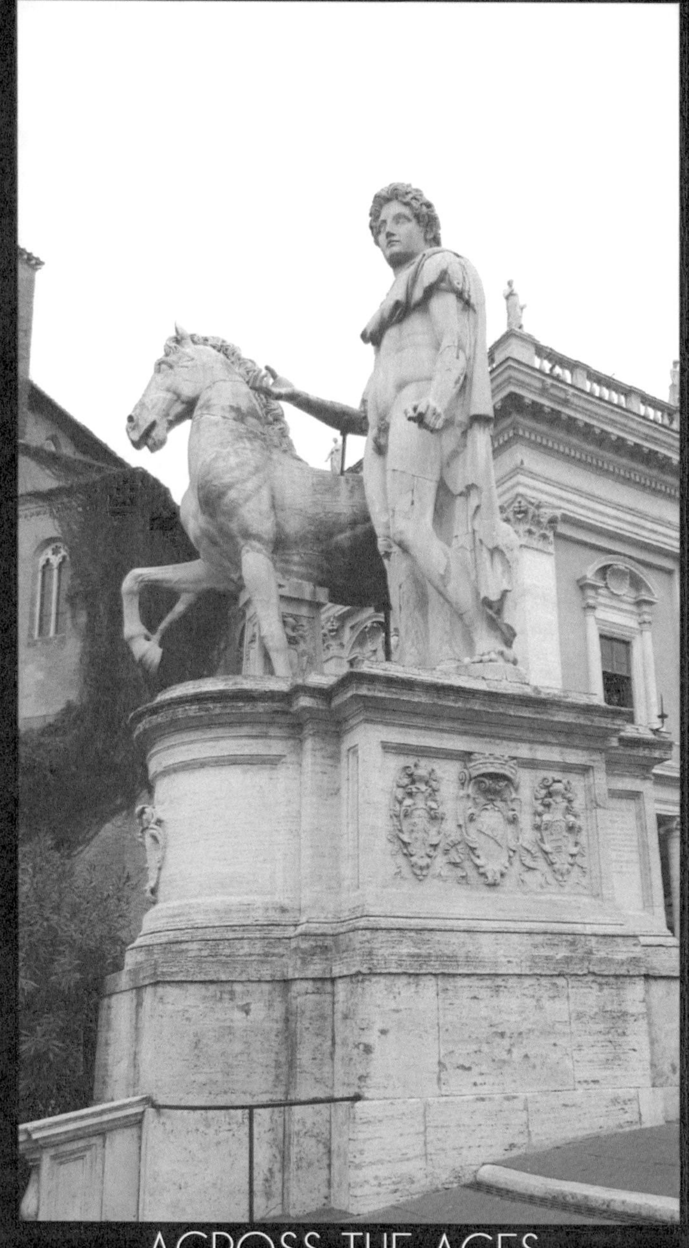

ACROSS THE AGES

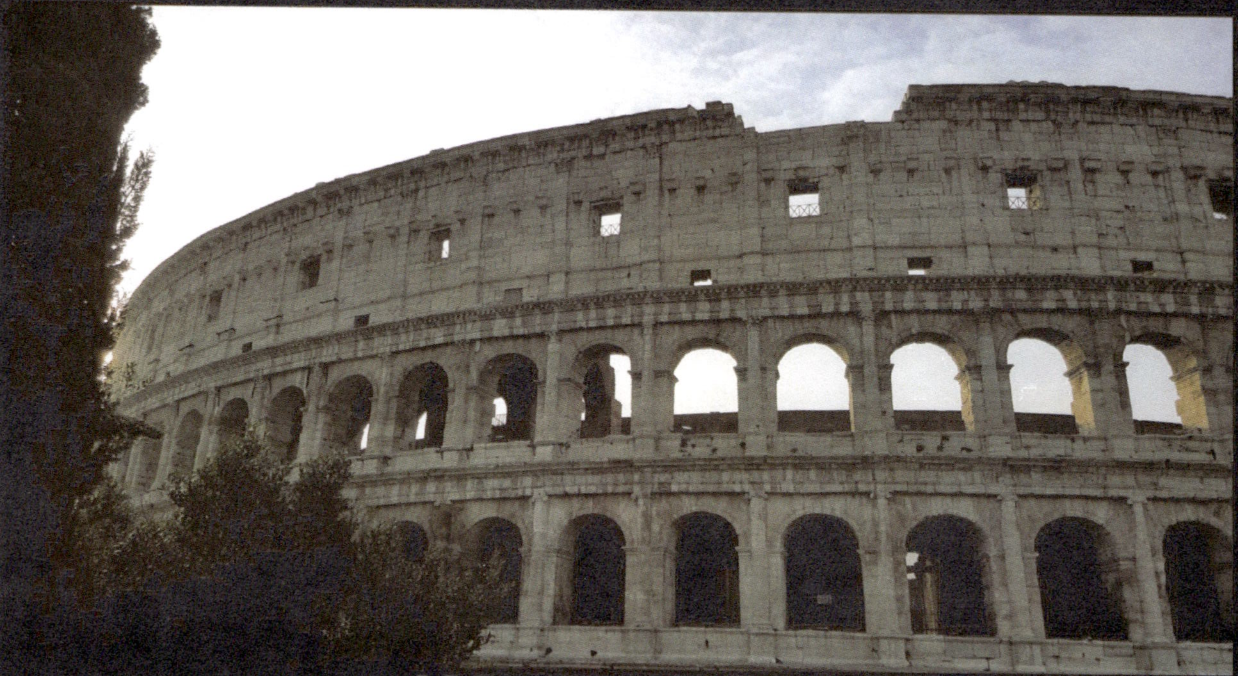

BREAKING CURVE

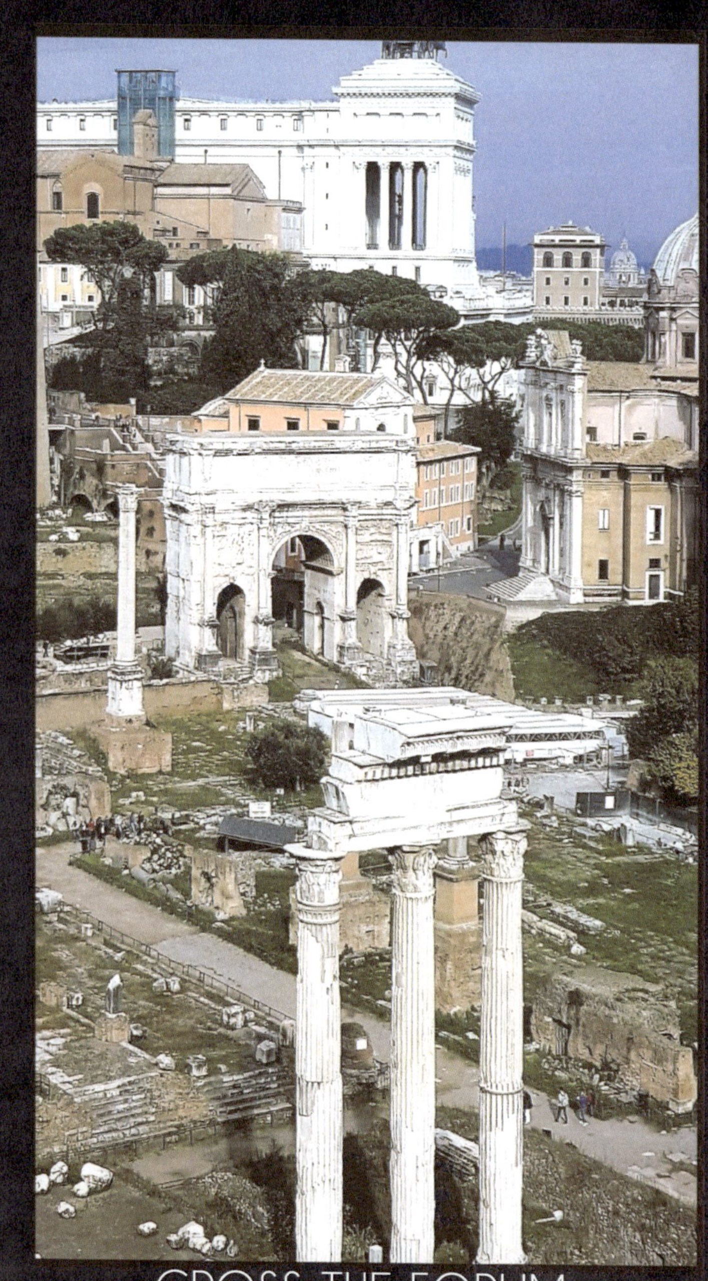

CROSS THE FORUM

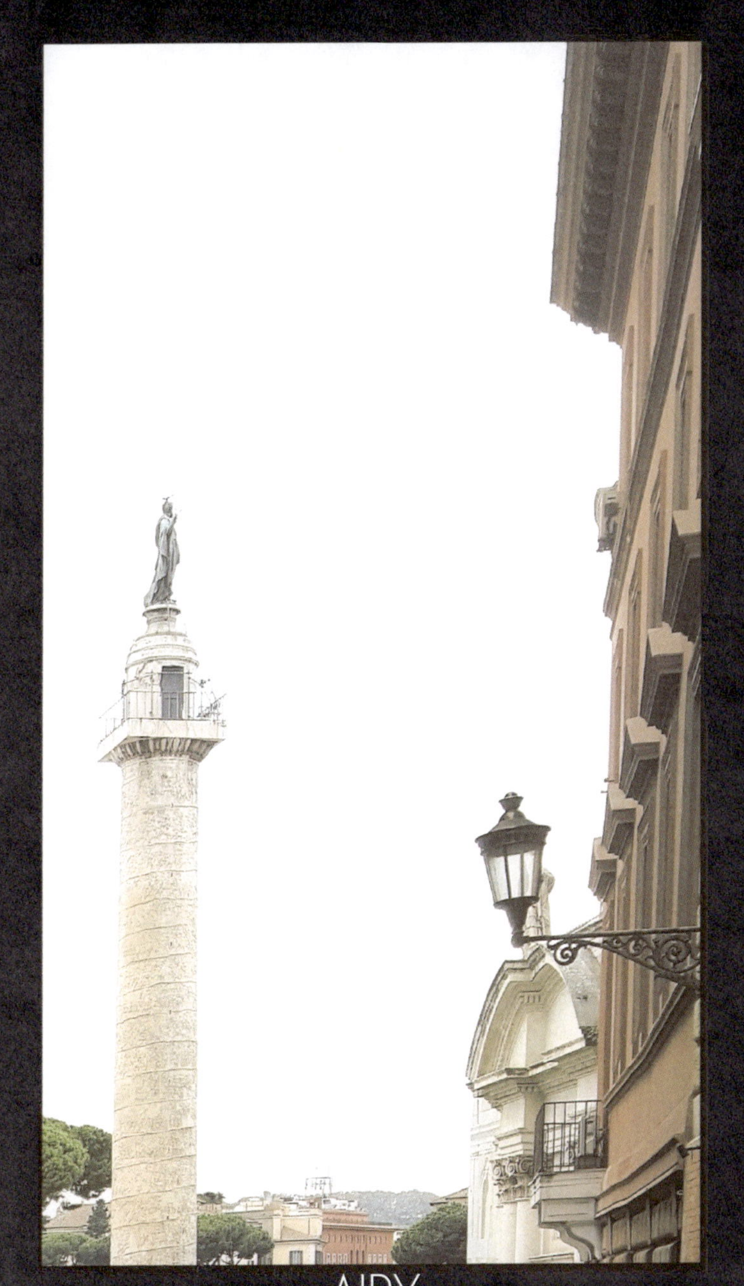

AIRY

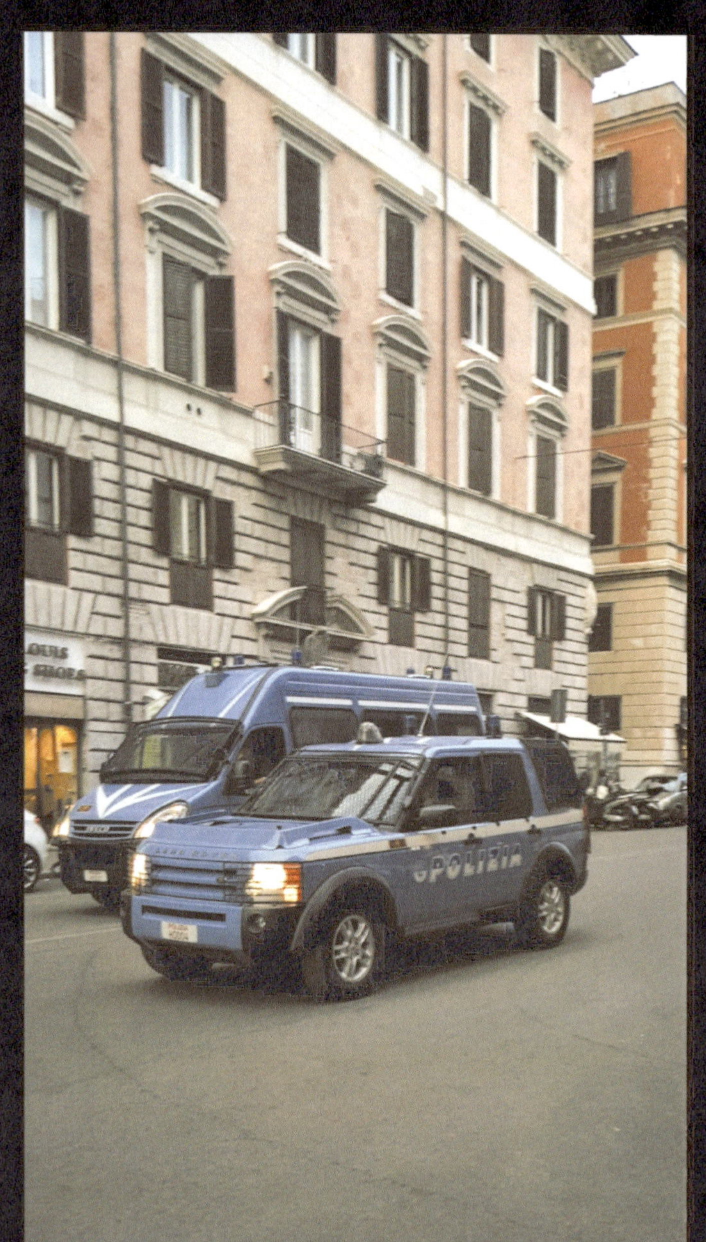

BOY/GIRL

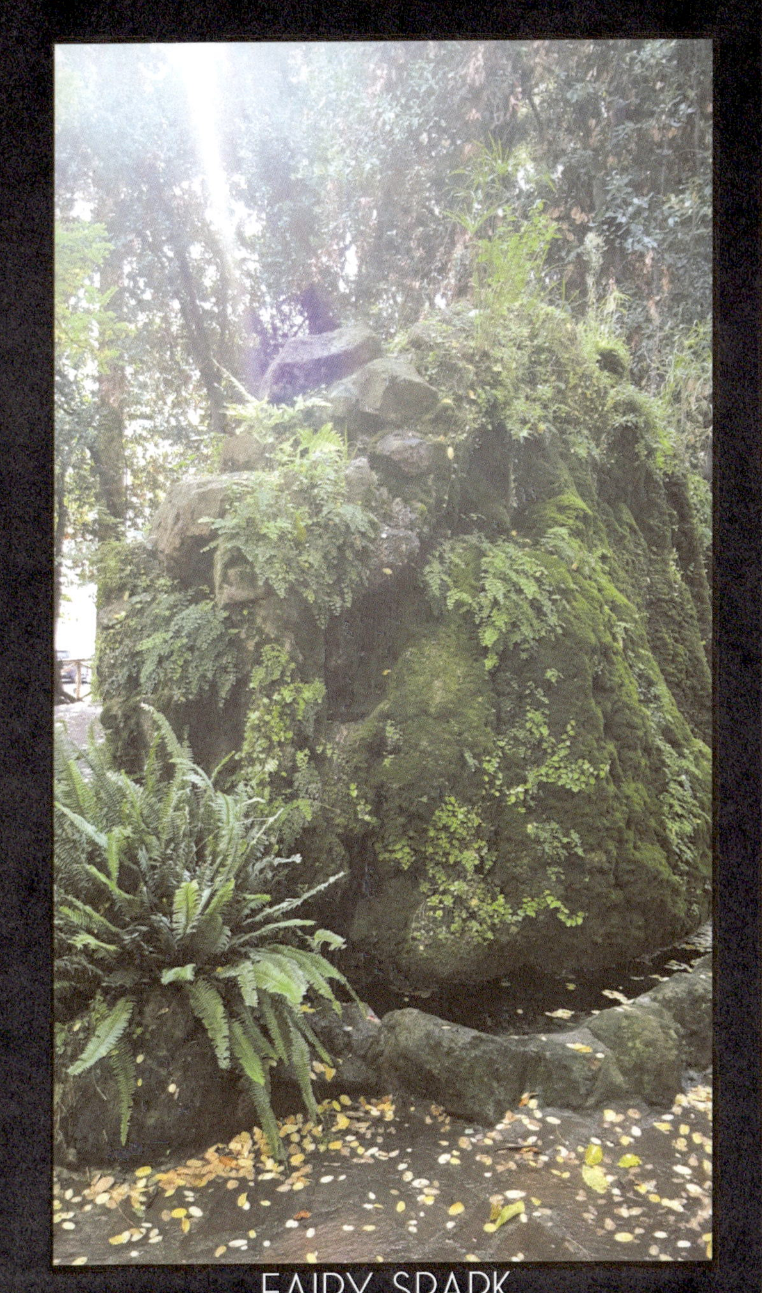

FAIRY SPARK

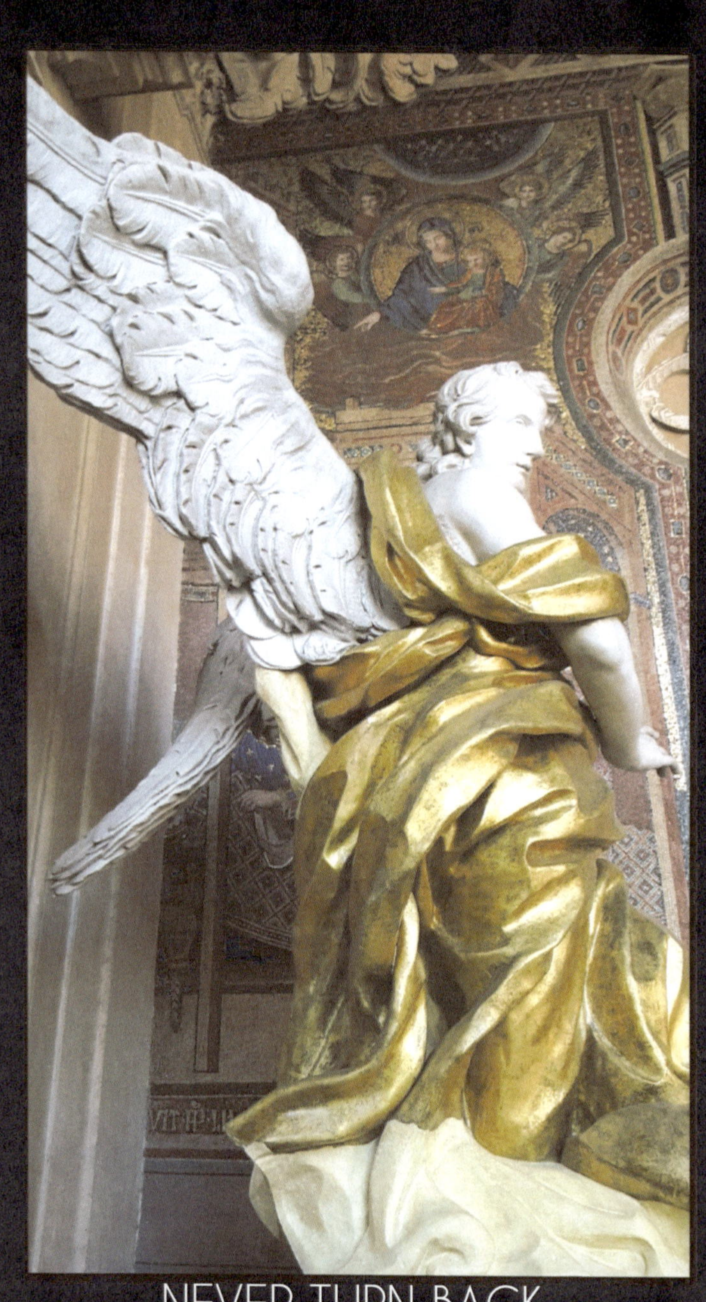

NEVER TURN BACK

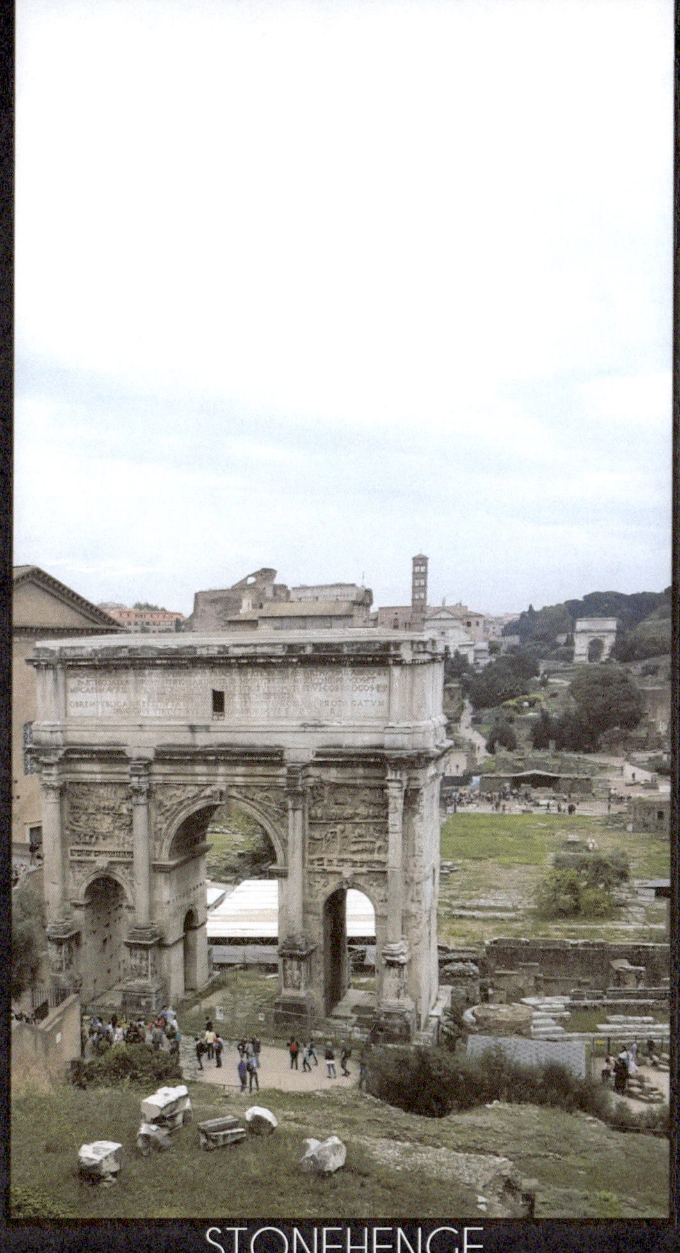

STONEHENGE

CATWALK

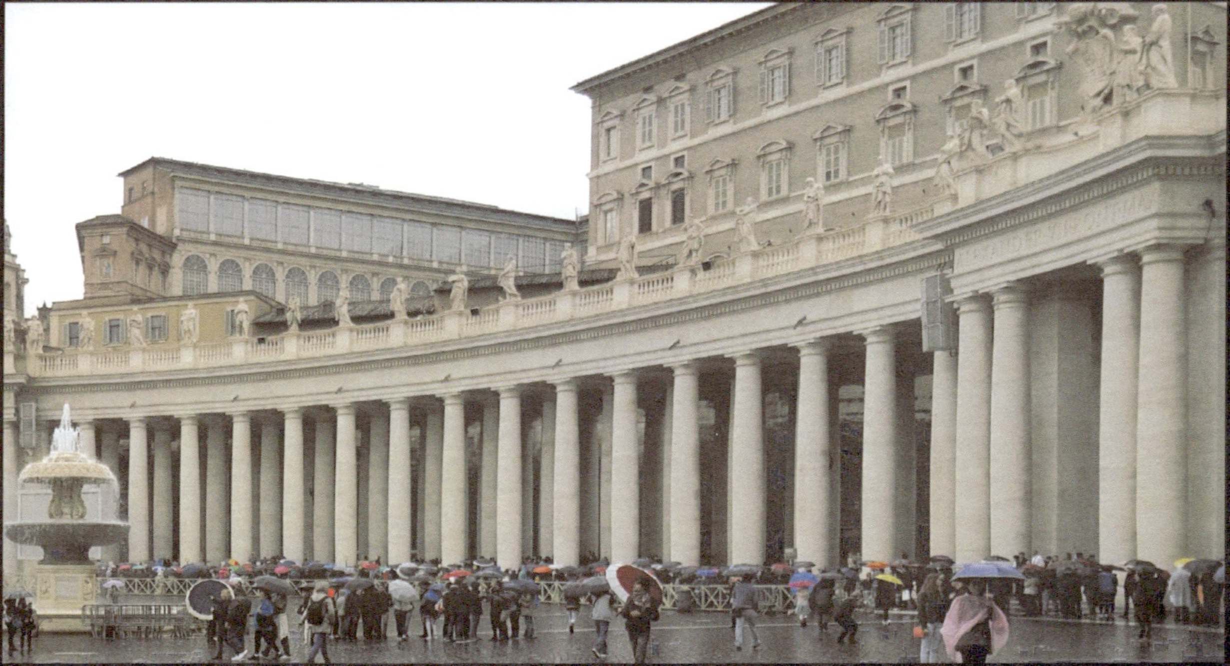

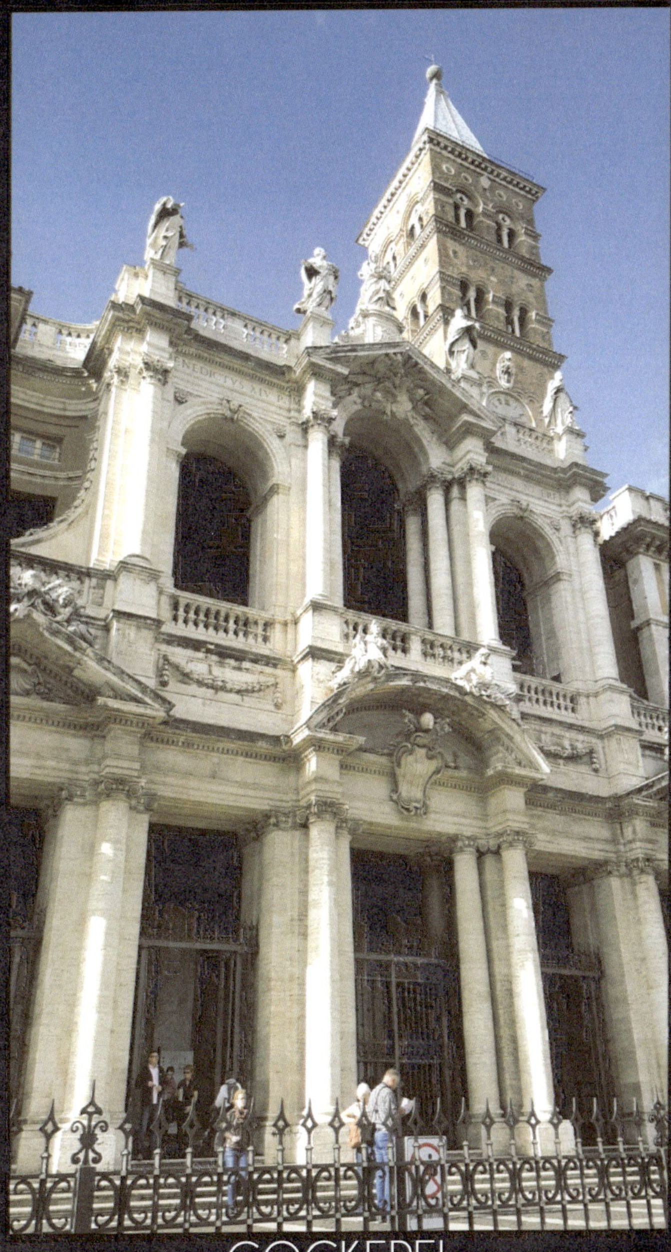

COCKEREL

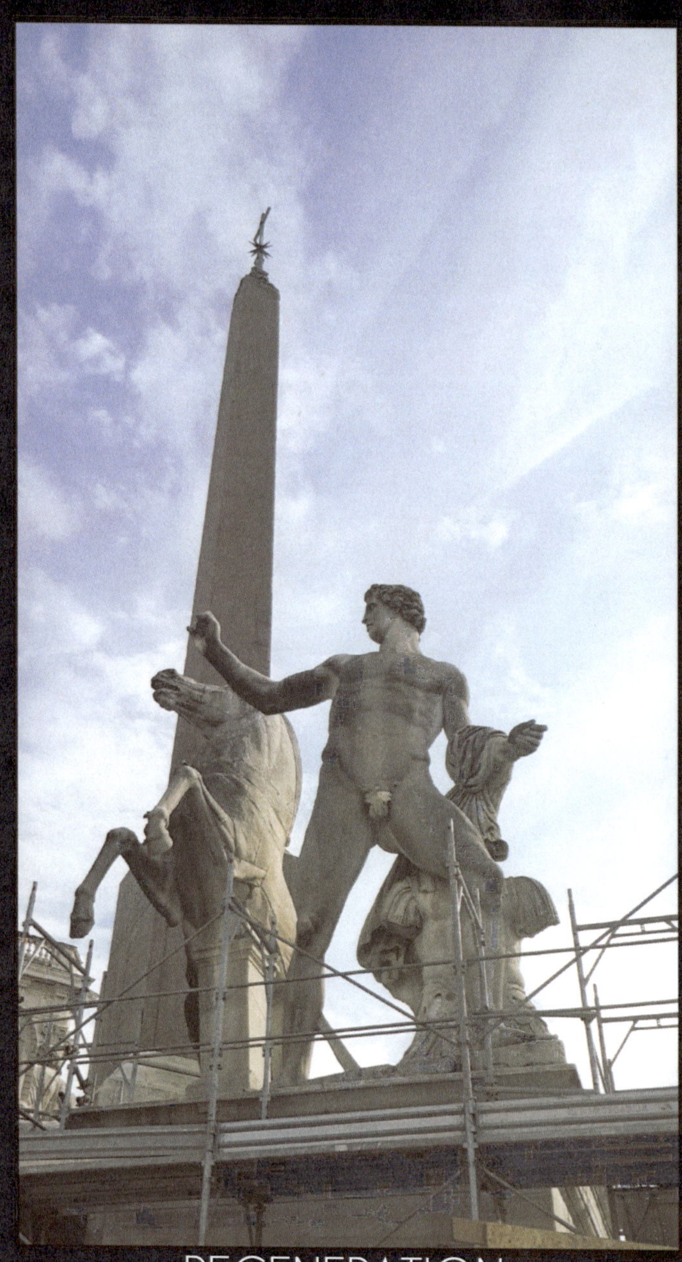

REGENERATION

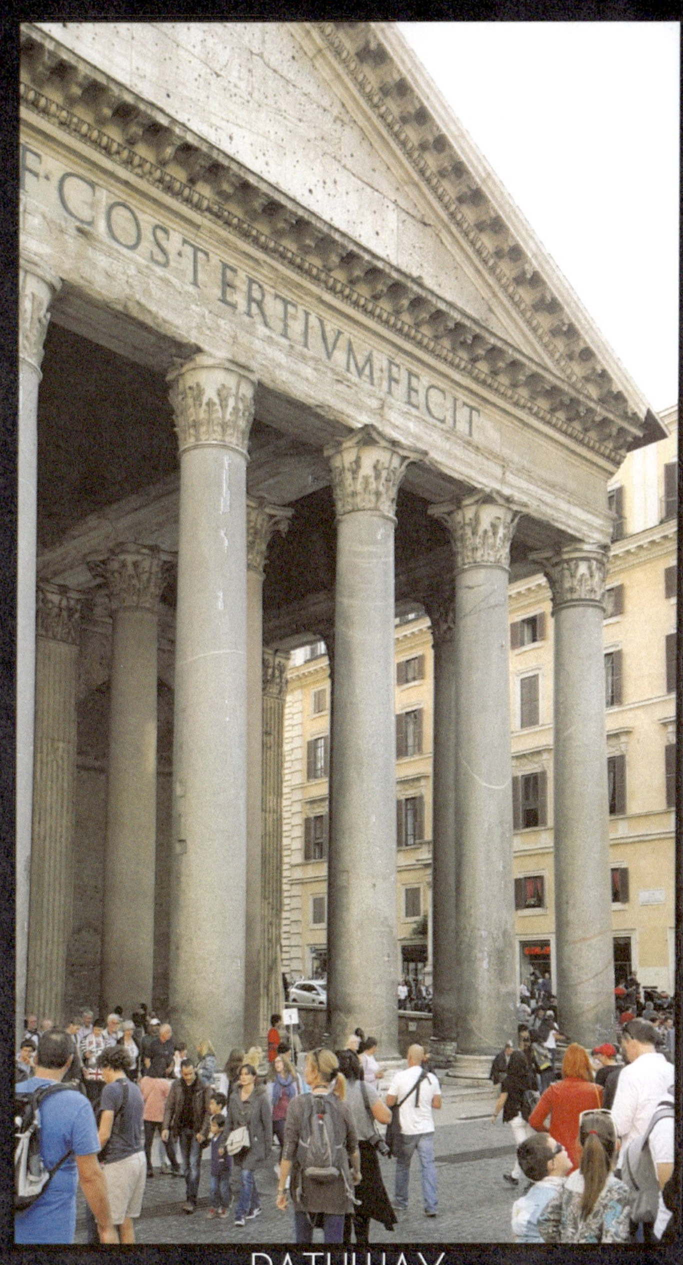

PATHWAY

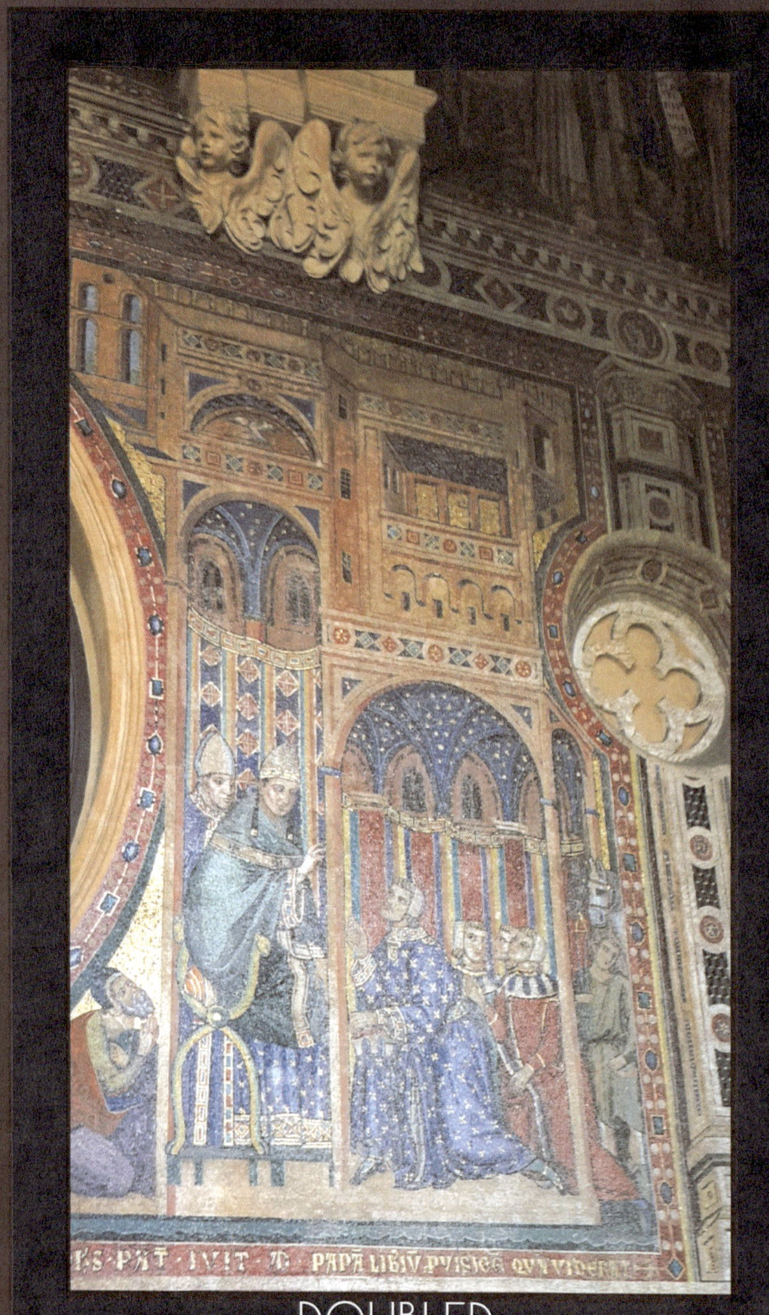

DOUBLED

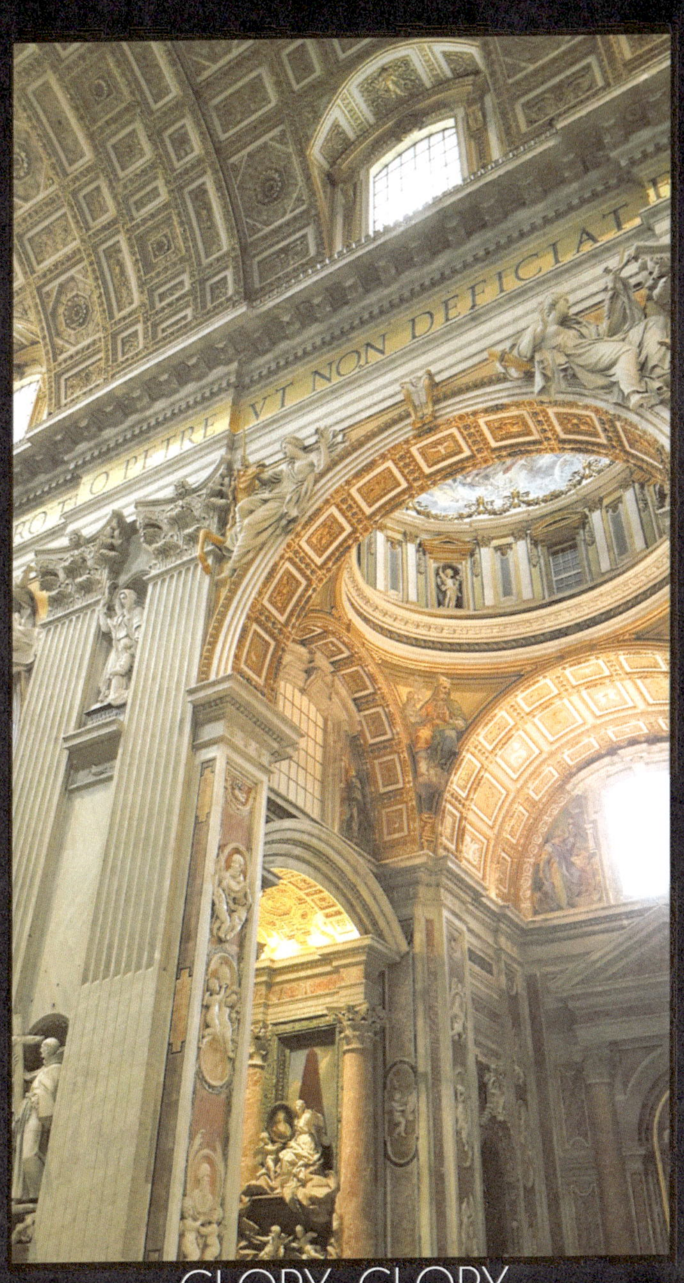

GLORY, GLORY

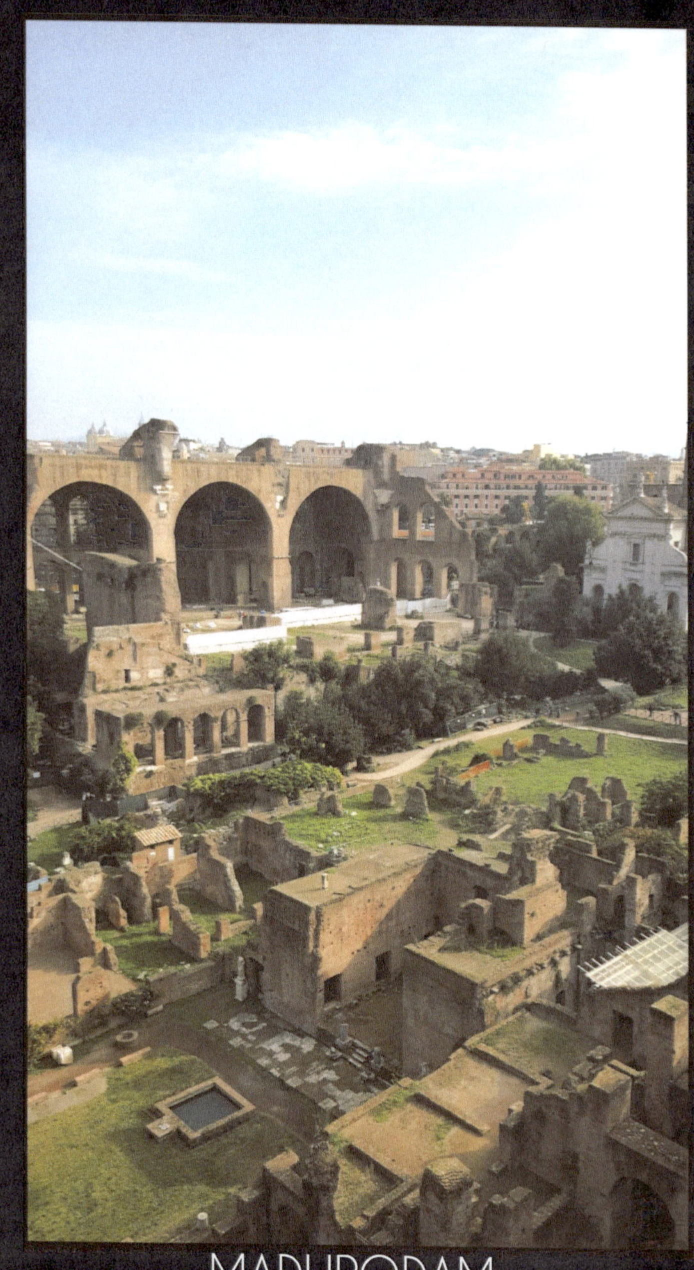

MADURODAM

RELEASE

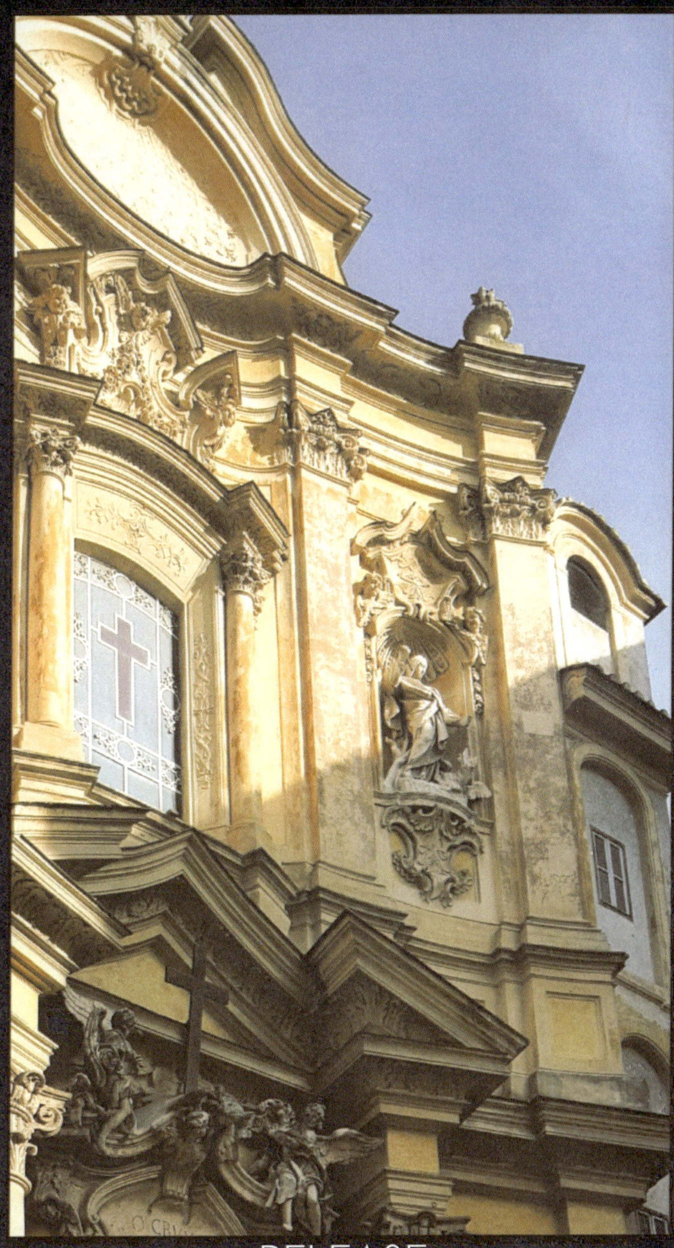

RELEASE

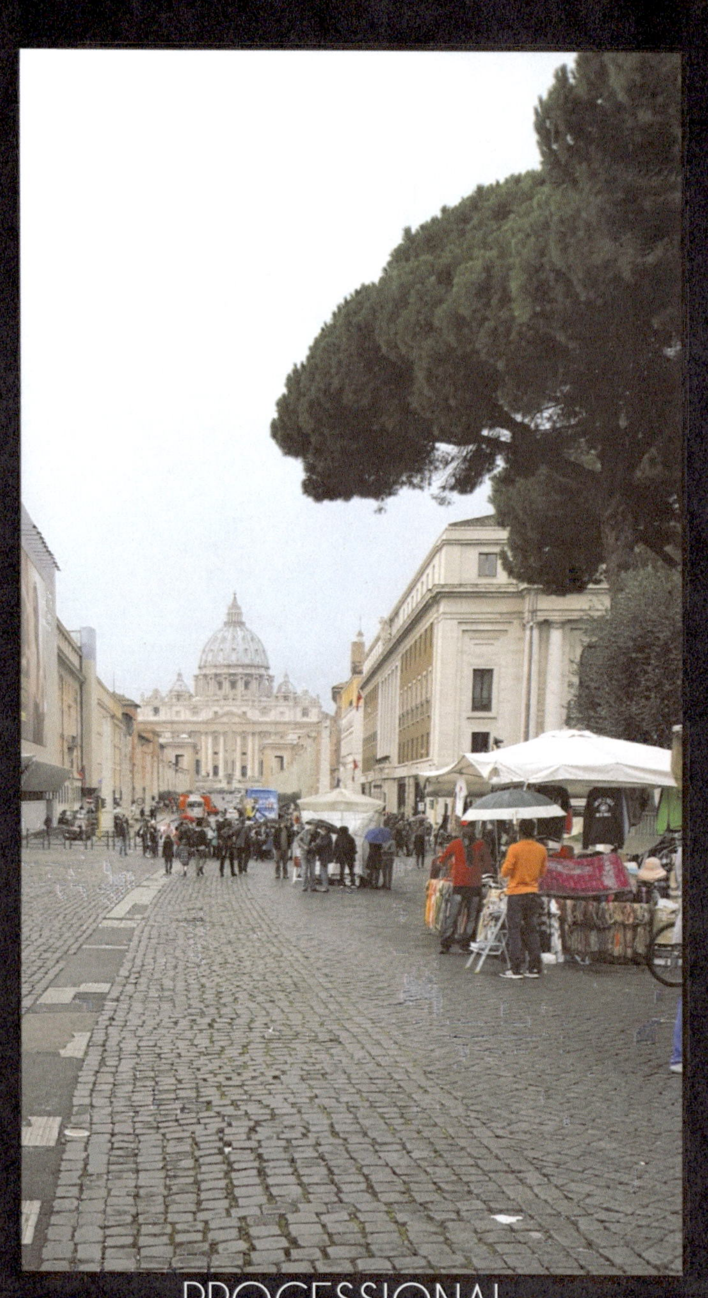

PROCESSIONAL

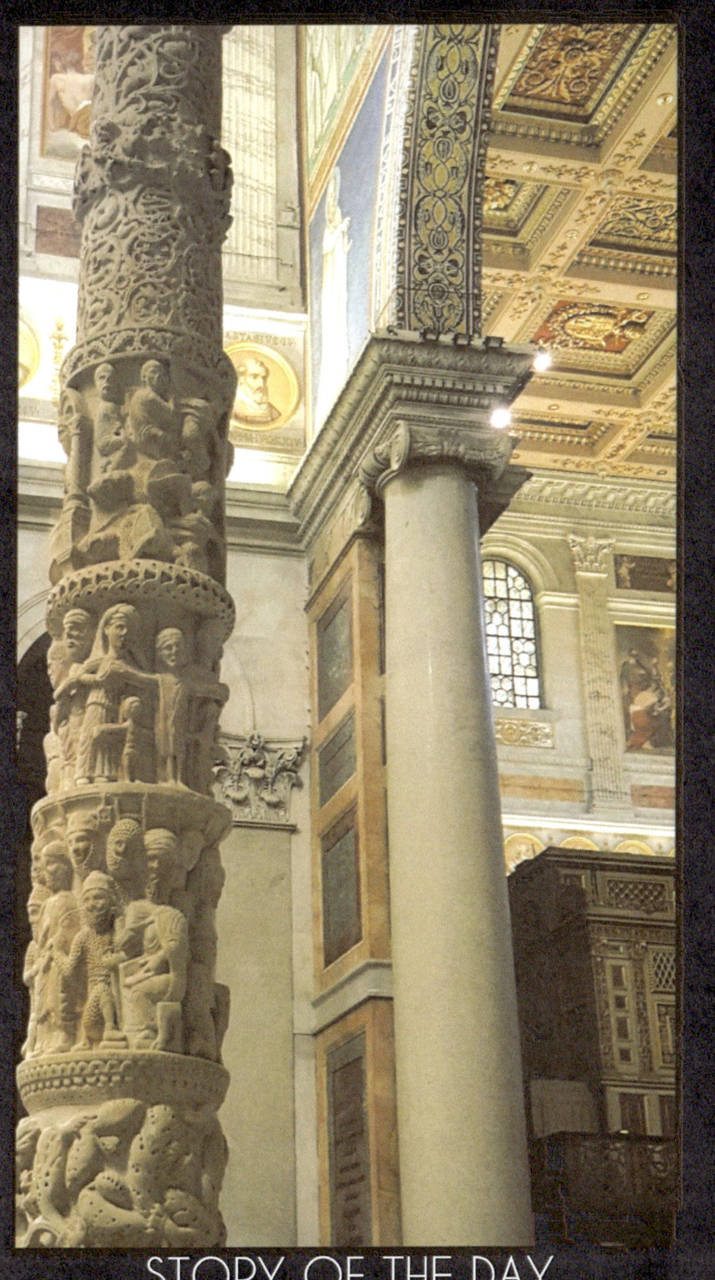

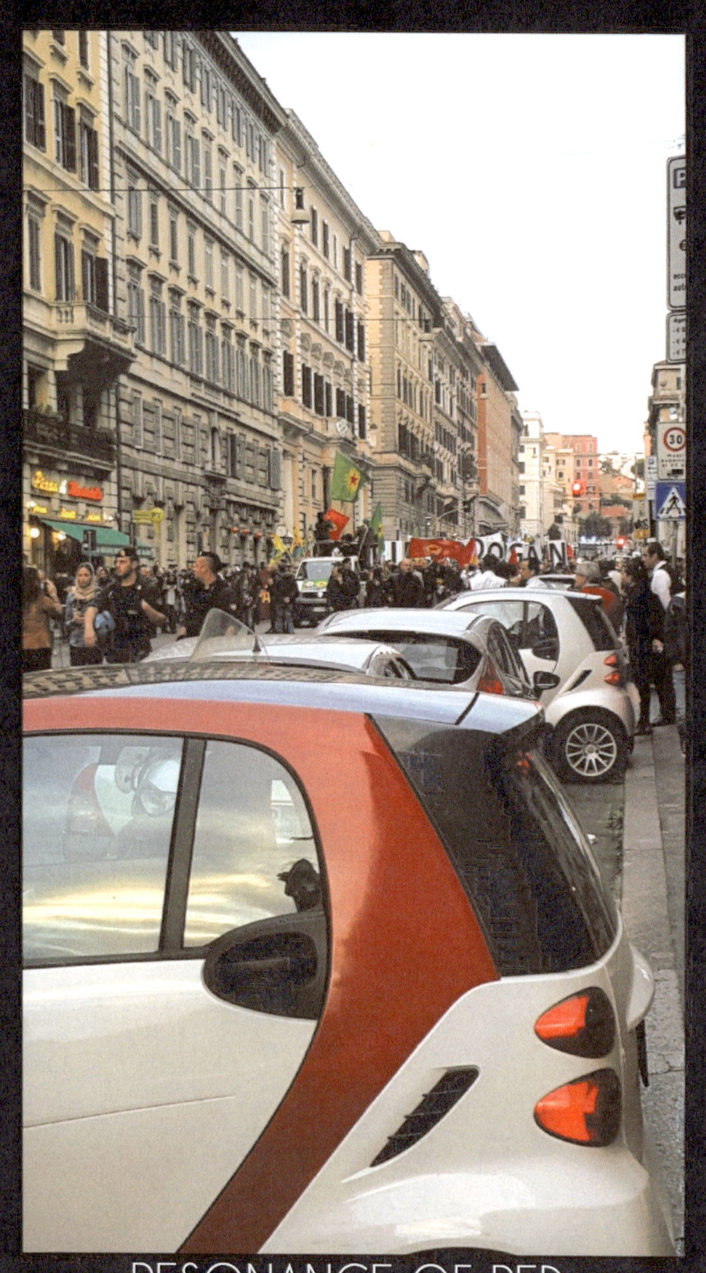

RESONANCE OF RED

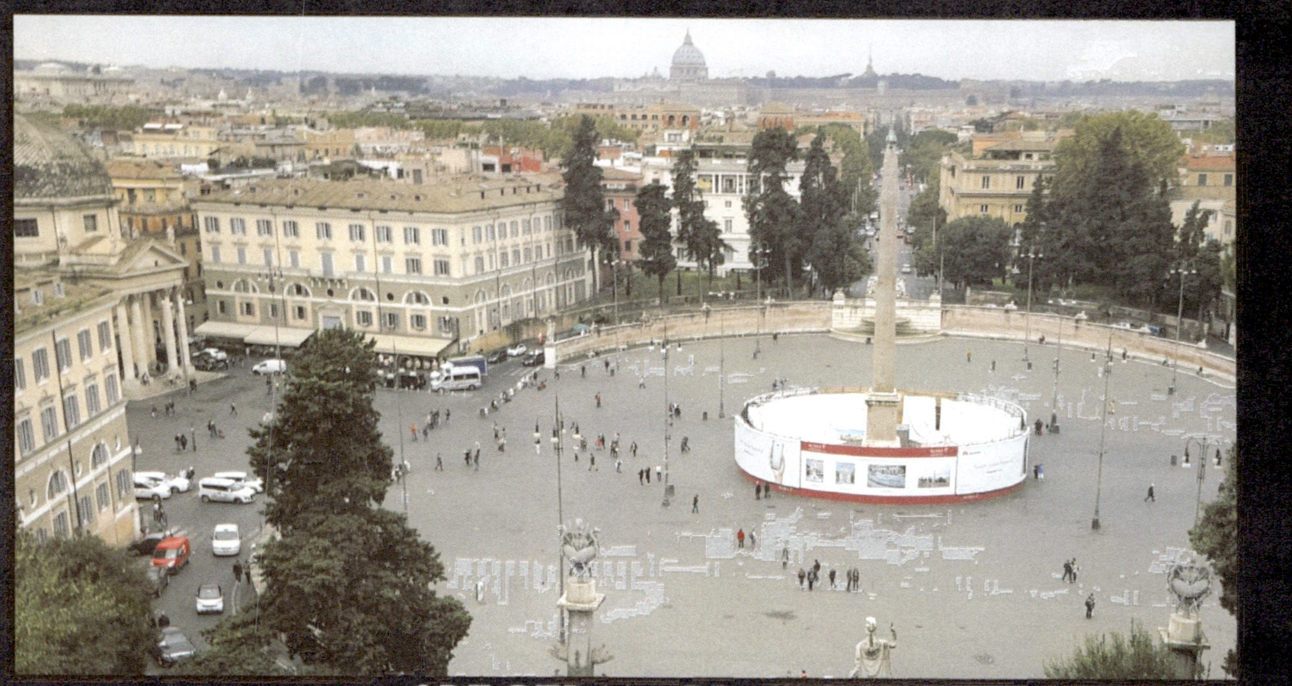
SPECTRAL GRAINS

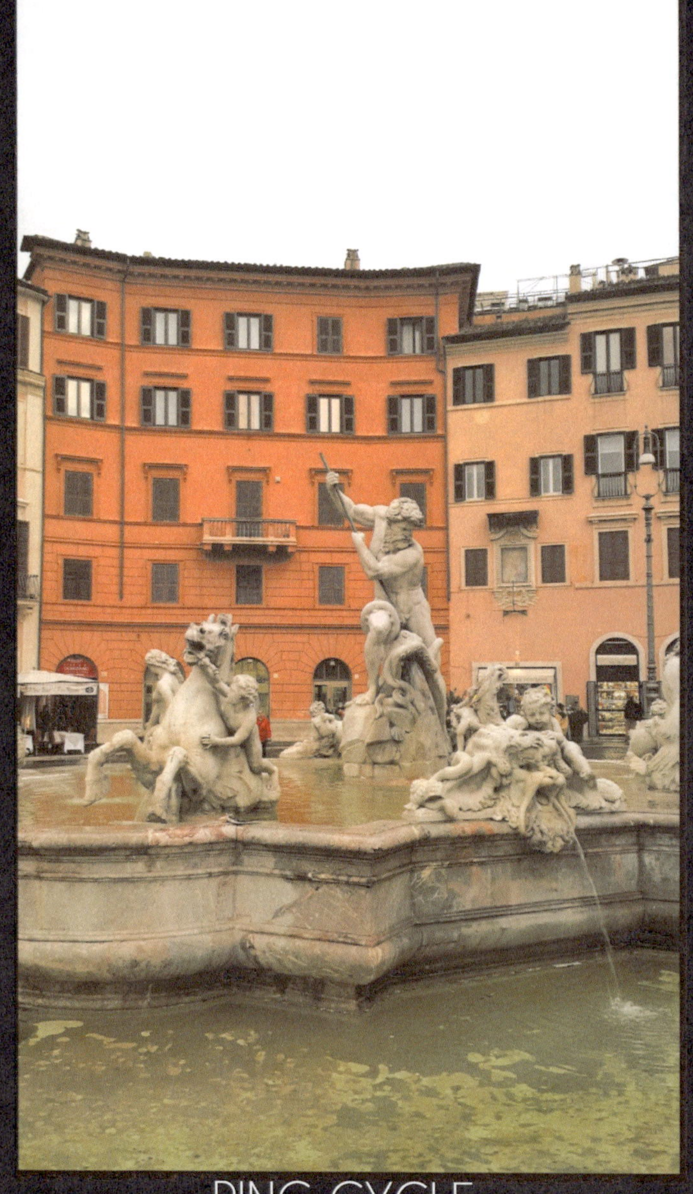

RING CYCLE

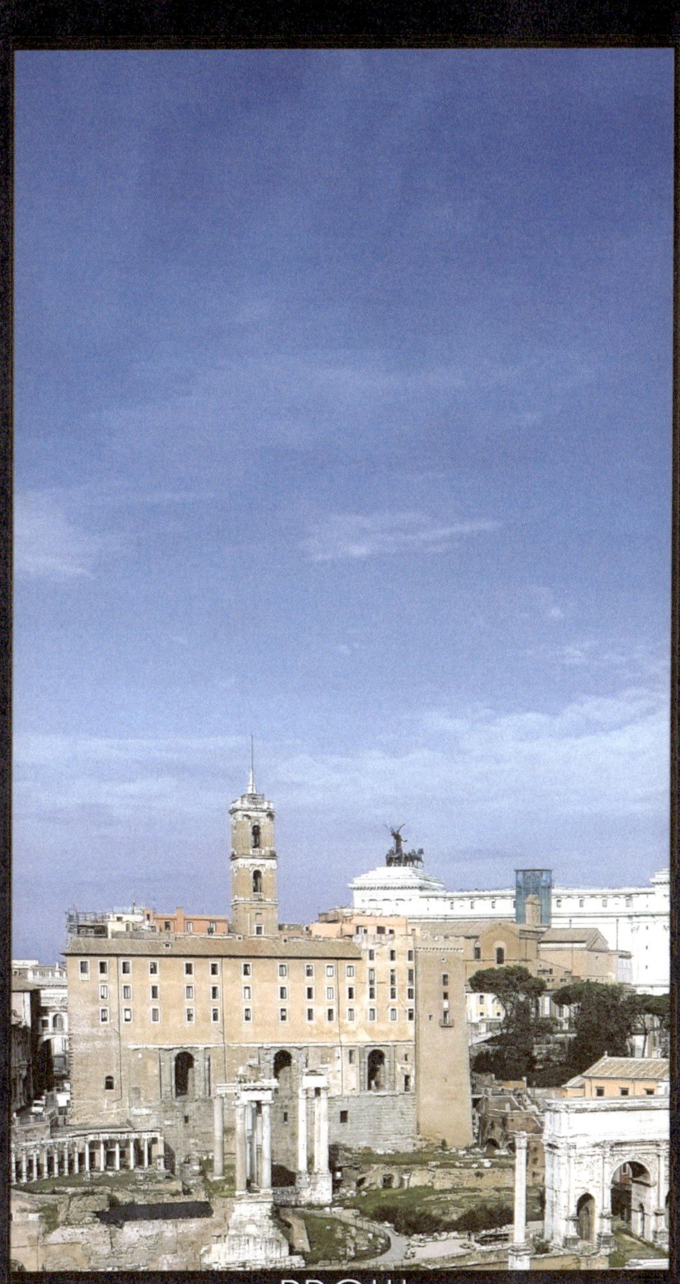

PROW

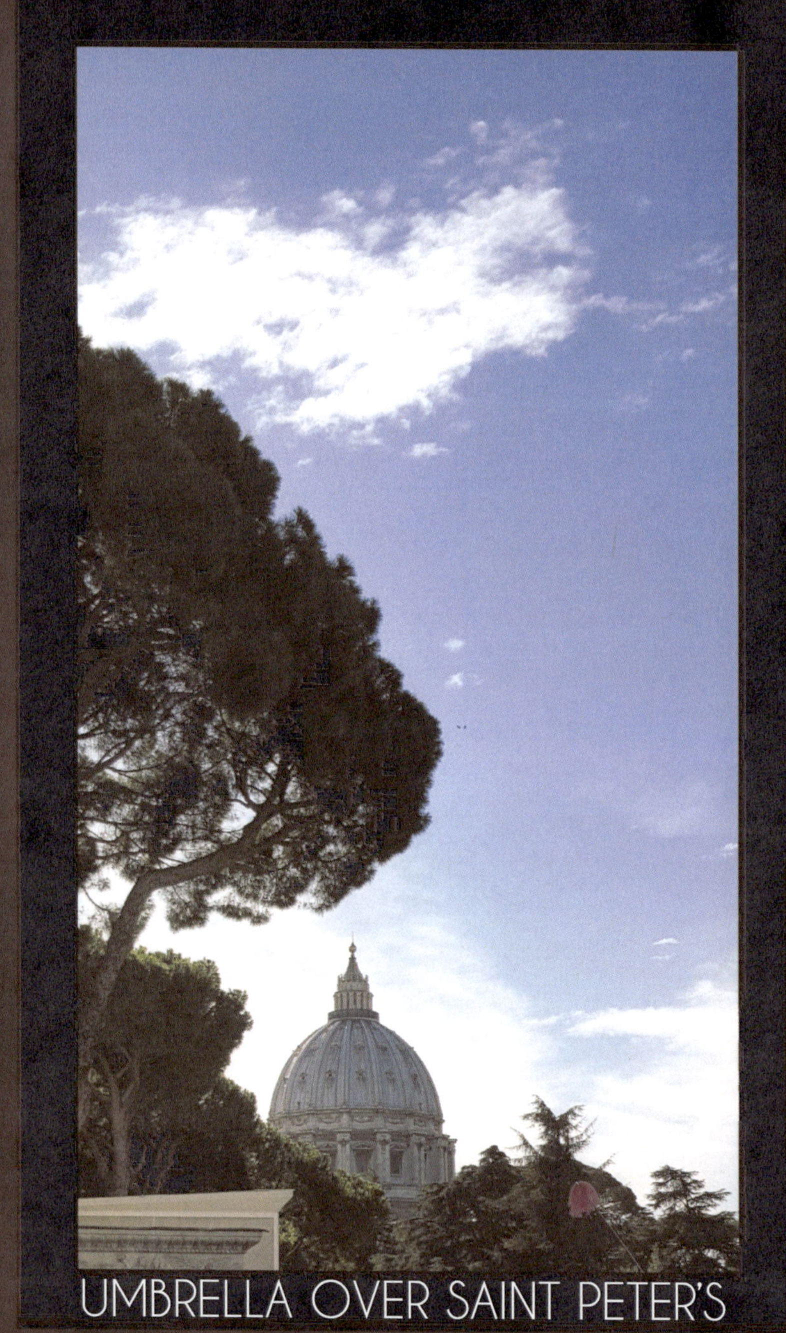
UMBRELLA OVER SAINT PETER'S

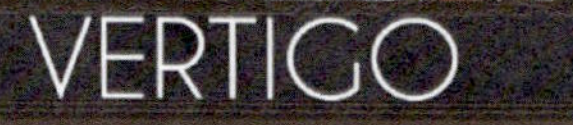

VERTIGO

GILDED PARADE

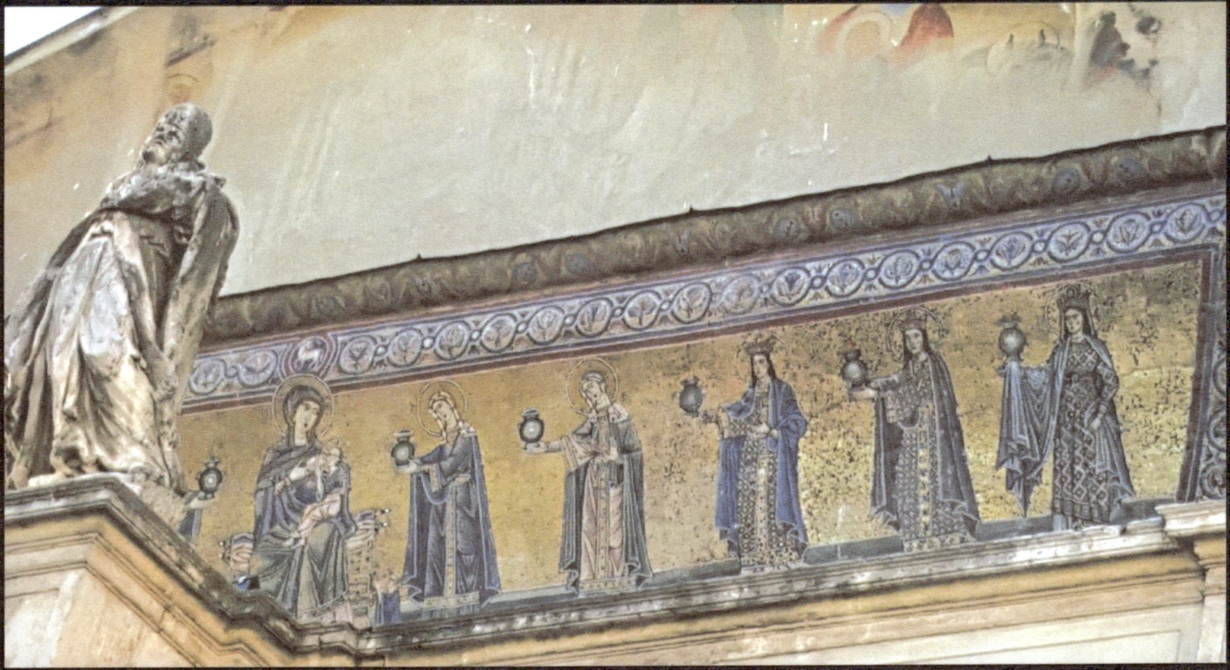

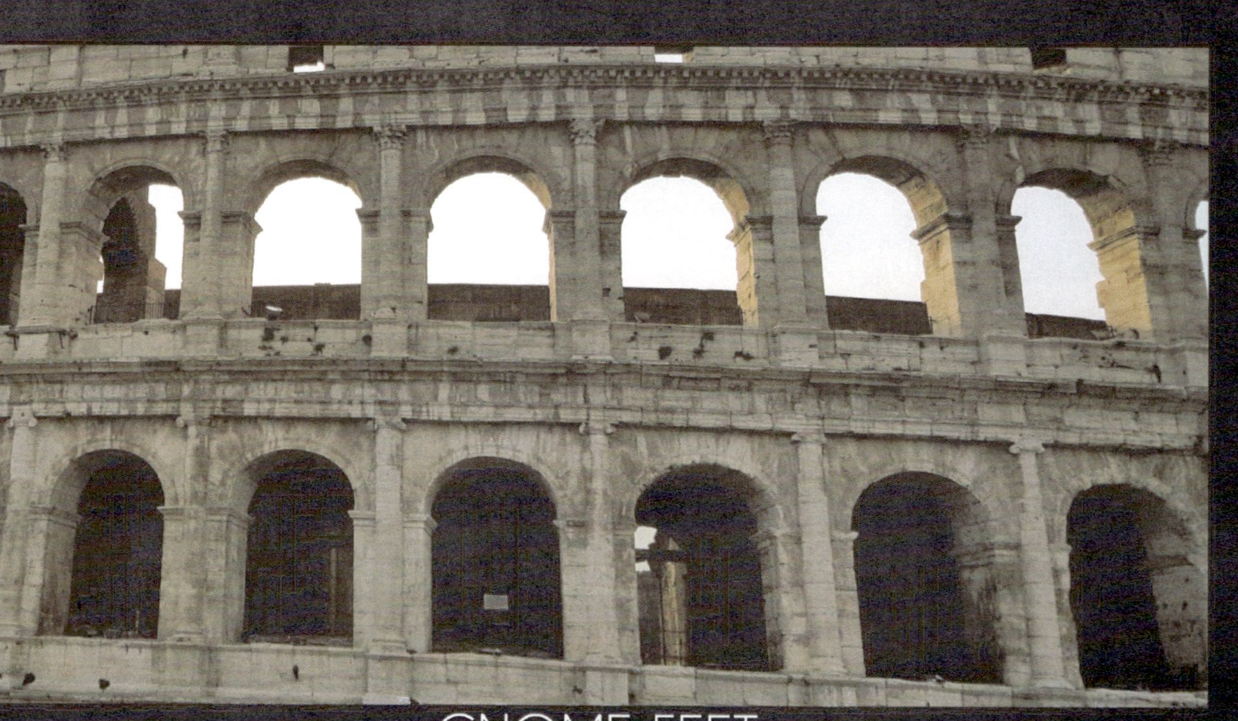

GNOME FEET

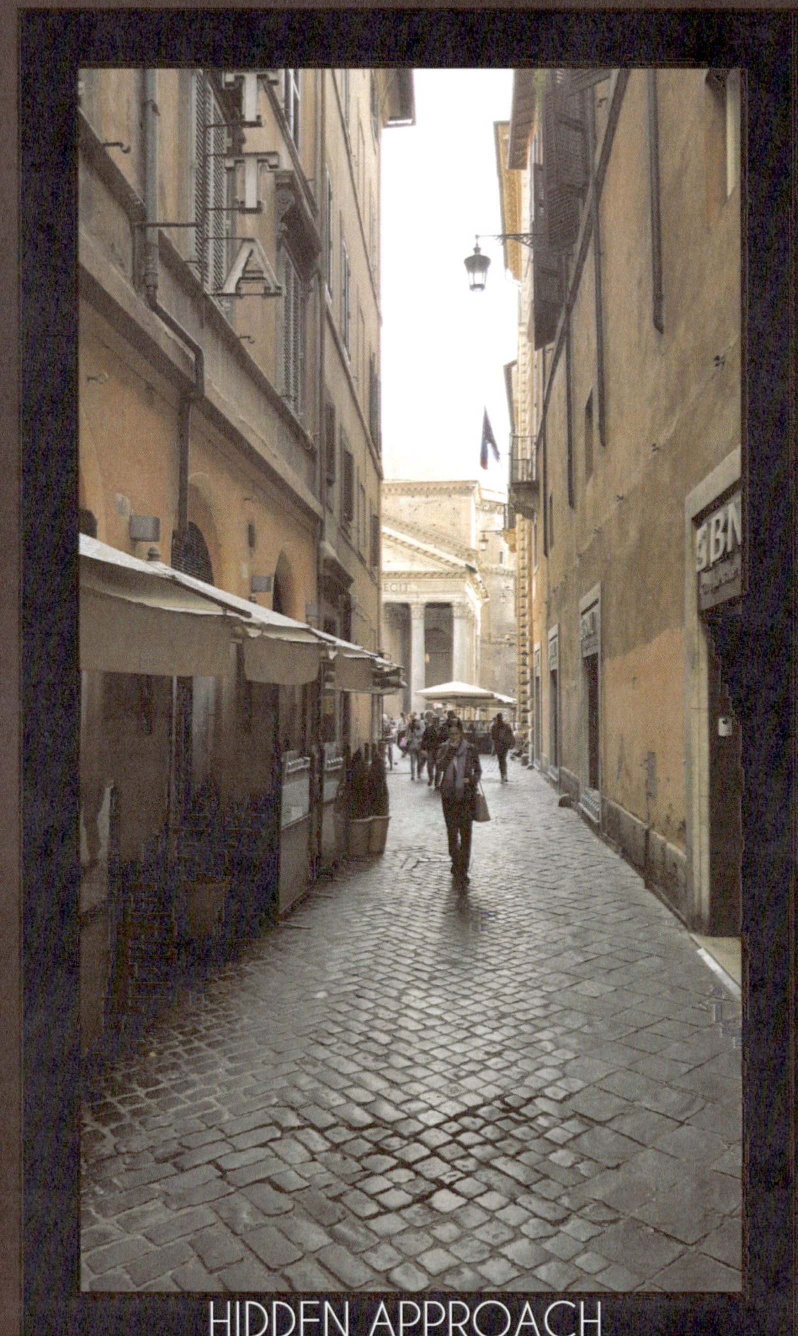

HIDDEN APPROACH

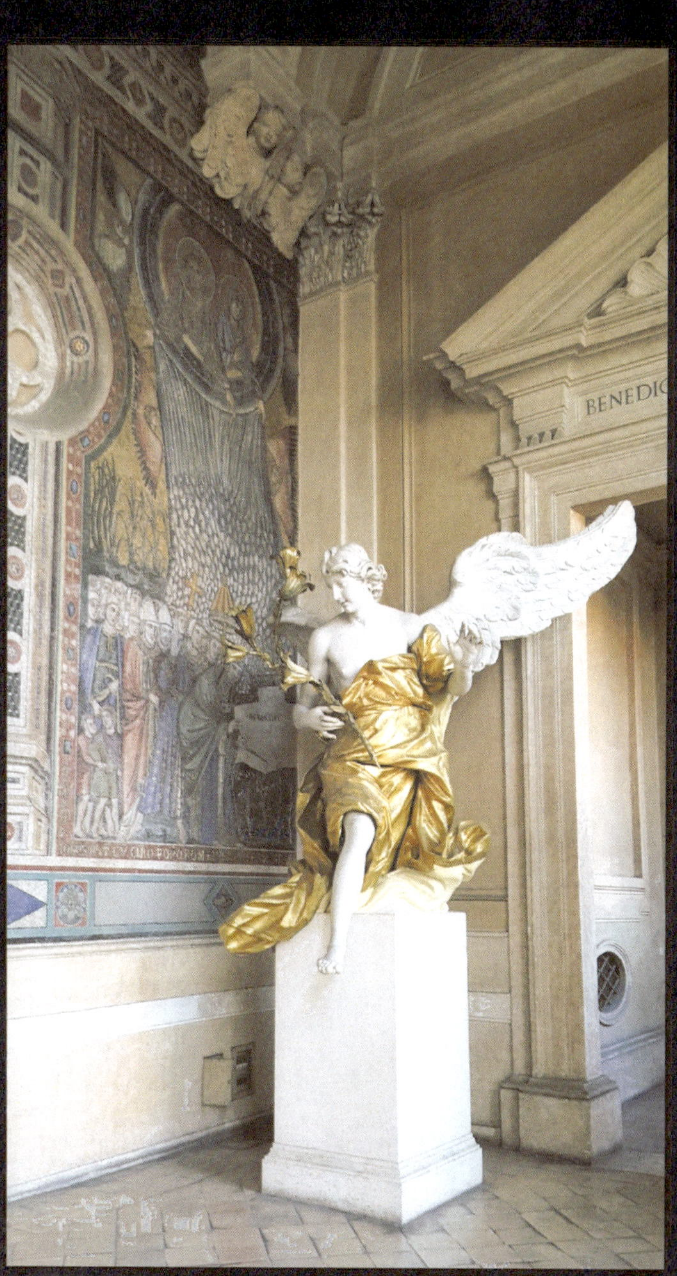

LEFT BEHIND

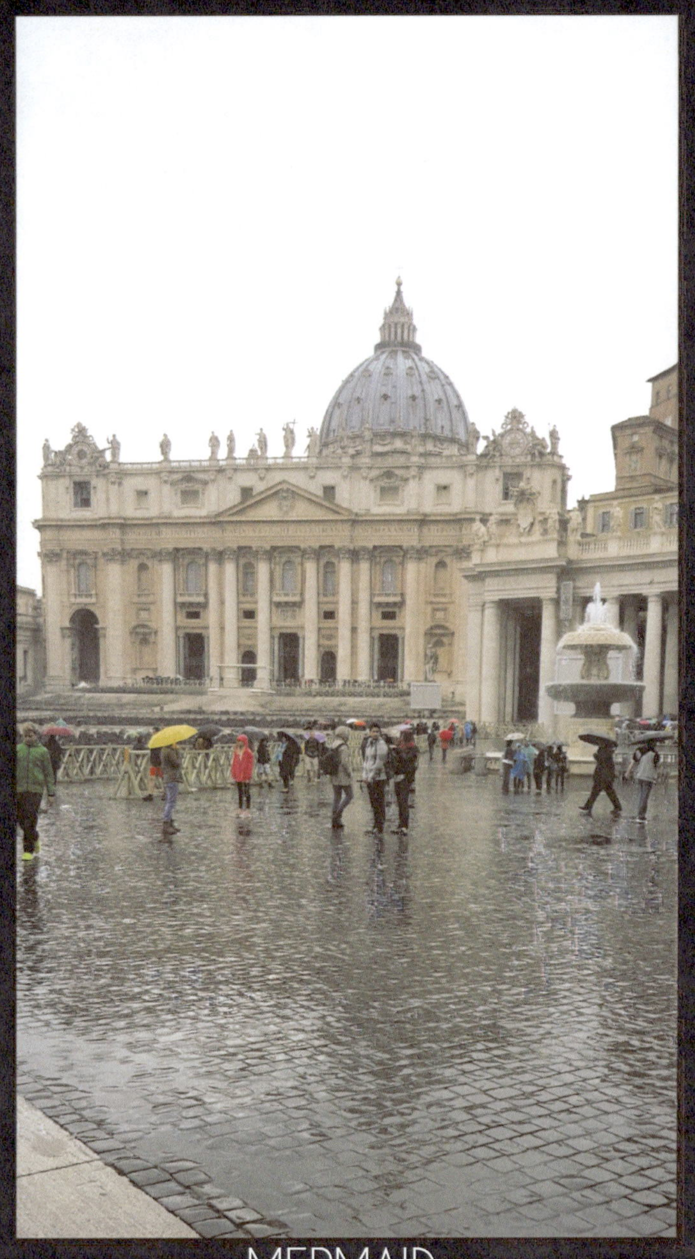

MERMAID

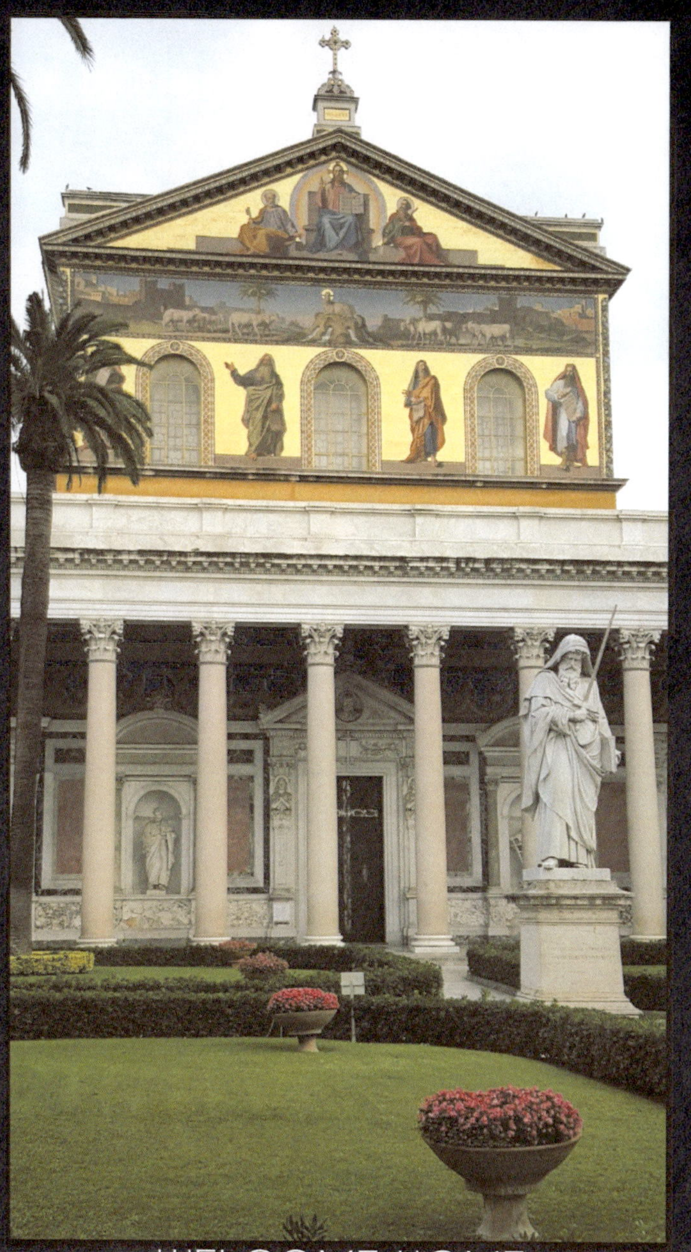

WELCOME HOME

About the Author

Laine Cunningham leads readers around the world. *The Family Made of Dust* is set in the Australian Outback, while *Reparation* is a novel of the American Great Plains. Her travel memoir *Woman Alone* appeals to fans of *Wild* and *Eat Pray Love*.

Novels by
Laine Cunningham

The Family Made of Dust

Beloved

Reparation

Other Books by
Laine Cunningham

Woman Alone: A Six-Month Journey Through the Australian Outback

On the Wallaby Track

Seven Sisters: Spiritual Messages from Aboriginal Australia

Writing While Female or Black or Gay

The Zen of Travel
The Zen of Gardening
Zen in the Stable
The Zen of Chocolate
The Zen of Dogs

Ruins of Rome I & II
Ancients of Assisi I & II
Panoramas of Portugal
Altitudes of the Alps
Flourishes of France
Portraits of Paris
Tableaus of Tbilisi
Grandeur in the Republic of Georgia
Paragons of Prague
Hidden Prague
Lidice Lives
Along the Via Appia
The Pillars of the Bohemian Paradise
Terezín and Theresienstadt
Garden City Garbatella
Captivating Capri
Notre Dame Cathedral
The Beauty of Berlin
Milan Cathedral
Treasures of Turin
Linger in Lisbon
The Splendors of Sintra
Spectacles of Stepantsminda
Marvels of Mtskheta

The Wisdom of Puppies
The Wisdom of Babies
The Wisdom of Weddings

The Beautiful Book of Questions
The Beautiful Book for Dream Seekers
The Beautiful Book for Rebels
The Beautiful Book for Women
The Beautiful Book for Lovers

* 9 7 8 1 9 4 6 7 3 2 3 9 2 *